A Career Day with a Scientist

Katie Smythe

Rosen REAL READERS

Rosen Classroom™
New York

A scientist is a person who tries to understand how things work. A scientist's job is to ask questions. They use experiments to answer those questions.

Some scientists study oceans and rivers. They take samples of the water. These scientists test the water for chemicals to make sure the water is clean.

Other scientists help find important materials trapped inside rocks. They help find materials we use every day like metal and oil.

This scientist studies plants. Plants are important to the planet. They use sunlight to make the air we breathe.

Scientists can work in a laboratory. Laboratories are places where experiments are made. They have the tools a scientist needs.

Safety is important during an experiment. Scientists wear gloves and coats to protect their skin.

This scientist uses a beaker to make a measurement. The scientist wears goggles. Goggles protect the scientist's eyes.

Scientists use microscopes. Microscopes make small objects look bigger. A scientist can see more with a microscope than with only her eyes.

Scientists write down what they see during an experiment. It is important to keep track of facts and measurements.

Scientists study and ask questions about the world. They try to make the world a better place. What would you do as a scientist?

Glossary

beaker A glass container for laboratory use.

energy Something that gives power.

experiment The steps a scientist takes to answer a question.

laboratory The place where scientists do their experiments.